RED
PANDAS

RED PANDAS

A Natural History

DORCAS MacCLINTOCK

Photographs by
ELLAN YOUNG

CHARLES SCRIBNER'S SONS · NEW YORK

All photographs by Ellan Young except those appearing on the following pages:
John L. Gittleman: pages 77 and 81.
William K. Sacco: pages 5, 6, 7, 8, 9, 11, 18, 65 and 66.
Pralad Yonzon: pages 22, 24, 26 and 28.

Charles Scribner's Sons Books for Young Readers
Macmillan Publishing Company
866 Third Avenue • New York 10022
Collier Macmillan Canada, Inc.

Printed in the United States of America
First Edition   10 9 8 7 6 5 4 3 2 1

Library of Congress Cataloging-in-Publication Data
MacClintock, Dorcas.
Red pandas : a natural history / Dorcas MacClintock ;
photographs by Ellan Young. — 1st ed.   p.   cm.
Bibliography: p.   Includes index.
Summary: Describes the physical characteristics, habitat,
behavior, and life cycle of the small long-tailed panda of Asia.
ISBN 0-684-18677-2
1. Ailurus fulgens—Juvenile literature. [1. Lesser panda. 2. Pandas.]
I. Young, Ellan, ill. II.Title.
QL737.C214M338   1988   88-3528
599.74′443—dc19   CIP
                                              AC

CONTENTS

To Miles S. Roberts and John L. Gittleman,
who have watched so many wahs and
have so generously shared their observations

1

The Original Panda

The Wah Itself

Wet snowflakes sifting down make it hard to see, but *look! There!* High up in the tree! Two red pandas peer down from their resting place. Their backs are white with snow.

The size of a very big house cat, a red panda has a large head, a short neck, a lithe body, and a long tail. Its round, short-muzzled, and charming face is topped by gently pointed ears that are lined, fringed, and tufted with fluffy white hairs. The muzzle is white and there is a white spot above each eye. Dark red-brown tear tracks run from the eyes over white cheeks to the corners of the mouth.

The panda's soft, loose-fitting coat is actually a double coat: a rusty red overcoat of inch-and-a-half-long moisture-shedding guard hairs and a dense undercoat of insulating gray-brown wool. Glossy brown-black fur marks the backs of its ears and covers throat, belly, and bearlike limbs.

The pads of the large paws are thickly furred. Like small, white-soled mukluks, they are protective footwear for pattering over snow and ice. The long, buffy-red tail, nearly two-thirds of the head-and-

1

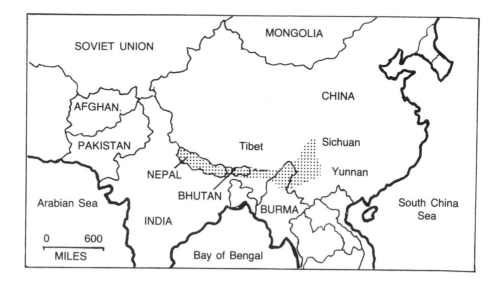

body length, has eight or nine more or less distinct dark red-brown bands and a dark tip and is so heavily furred that it appears cylindrical.

Red pandas live in temperate forests from Nepal eastward along the Himalaya through the high mountains of northern Burma, and into China: southwestern Tibet, and western Yunnan and Sichuan provinces.

For nearly half a century after it was named, the red panda was *the* panda. Then, in 1869, Père Armand David, a Jesuit missionary-naturalist, saw at last the "famous white-and-black bear," and another animal became known as the giant panda. The original panda, being smaller, came to be called the lesser panda, but red panda is the name preferred for this most captivating of **carnivores.***

There are other names, some given by European naturalists—shining panda, red cat bear, Himalayan raccoon, and fire fox—and some that are native names: *ye, nigalya ponya, thokya, wakdonka, sankam, woker, chitwa, khunda,* and *wah.*

In this book about the red panda, the animal usually will be referred to as panda or wah.

---

*Words in boldface type are defined in the glossary beginning on page 95.

Early Accounts

MAJOR GENERAL THOMAS HARDWICKE

In 1821 an Englishman in the Indian Civil Service, Major General Thomas Hardwicke, described an unusual animal that lived in "the Himalaya chain of hills between Nepaul [sic] and the snowy mountains." Its body, he wrote, "is a beautiful fulvous brown colour" and "its haunts are about rivers and mountain-torrents." Hardwicke's paper, the first description of the red panda, was read at a November meeting of the Linnaean Society of London. Hardwicke intended to name the animal when he published his paper.

When Hardwicke's paper appeared in volume 15 of the society's *Transactions* for 1827, however, it was accompanied by a footnote by the society's secretary, stating that the author, while working on the paper, had come upon a recently published description of *Ailurus fulgens,* the very animal he expected to describe and name himself. The name Hardwicke had in mind was therefore "suppressed," but "the remainder of the paper is too important to be omitted."

Hardwicke included detailed drawings of the paws and teeth and he wrote that the animal was "frequently discovered by its loud cry or call, resembling the word *wha* [wah]. . . ."

NATHANIEL WALLICH

A botanist from Calcutta, collecting in the mountains of Nepal, had supplied the specimens described by Hardwicke. Nathaniel Wallich, probably the first European to see wahs in the wild, also collected animals for Alfred du Vaucel of the Museum of Natural History in Paris.

FRÉDÉRIC CUVIER

When the crates of specimens arrived in the museum, the zoologist Frédéric Cuvier, who was du Vaucel's father-in-law, must have been elated to find the skin and skeleton of a small "fire-colored cat."

Cuvier lost no time in adding the animal to his nearly finished chapter, part of a natural history of mammals* that appeared in 1825, four years after Hardwicke's paper had been read and two years before its publication.

After noting the significance of this new animal, Cuvier describes in detail its raccoonlike teeth, its fur (remarkable for its colors), and its body and tail, "like those of a large domestic cat."

Cuvier found the new animal a "beautiful species, one of the handsomest of known quadrupeds," and decided it belonged to the raccoon family, the **Procyonidae.** He called it the Bright Panda and provided its scientific name:

> I propose for the generic name . . . *Ailurus,* on account of its exterior resemblance to the cat and for its specific name that of *Fulgens,* because of its brilliant colours.

The illustration of a rotund red panda that accompanies Cuvier's account of *Ailurus fulgens* was reproduced in many of the animal treatises of the late 1800s.

---

*Geoffroy Saint-Hilaire, Etienne, *Histoire Naturelle des Mammifères,* avec des figures originales, colorées, desinées d'après des animaux vivants. (Paris, 1825.) 2:1-3, Plate 203.

BRIAN HOUGHTON HODGSON

The man who knew most about wahs was Brian Houghton Hodgson, another Englishman in the Indian Civil Service. In 1820 he was appointed assistant to the Resident in Nepal, a country then newly defined after years of strife between the British and mountain tribesmen, the Gurkhas. At heart a naturalist and a passionate collector, Hodgson soon had native people bringing him animals of all kinds.

By 1834 Hodgson had become British Resident in Nepal and was much involved in political struggles between India and Britain, but he found time to present a collection of mammals to the Zoological Society of London. His gift is acknowledged in the *Proceedings* of that year. Among the twenty-two species, "several of which were first made known to science by the exertions of Mr. Hodgson," is *Ailurus fulgens*.

The year before, Hodgson had sent "a full and careful description of the habits and of the hard and soft anatomy of *Ailurus*" to the Zoological Society. Apparently the manuscript had been lost. Hodgson was annoyed that his British colleagues ignored his account:

> I pointed to my own drawings, specimens, and description of the structure and habits of *Ailurus* lying unused in their hands whilst their Journal was putting forth the mere crumbs gathered from Cuvier's table. . . .

Hodgson not only knew a great deal more about wahs than did Cuvier, who had never seen the animal alive, but he had a hands-on familiarity with them. Having "little speed, cunning, or ferocity," wahs, he found, were easily captured. "I . . . have kept several for a year or two . . . feeding them on rice and milk . . . or eggs, all of which they like. . . ."

Hodgson's paper "On the cat-toed subplantigrades of the sub-Himalayas" was published in the *Journal of the Asiatic Society of Bengal* in 1847. By then he had retired from his government post and lived in the hill station of Darjeeling. There, "in a narrow clearing of

majestic forest that then clothed the mountains of Sikkim . . . and crept up to the very walls of the few houses of which the station consisted,"* he devoted his time to the study of the Himalaya, its geography, its mammals and birds, and its peoples.

Hodgson was a competent draftsman and taught some of his native collectors to draw. An original watercolor of a wah, standing and in two sleeping positions, is among the Hodgson papers and drawings in the library of the Zoological Society of London. The young wah is life-size. The folio-size sheet includes anatomical sketches of two stomachs and various penned and penciled notes and measurements.

---

*Sir Joseph Hooker. In *Life of Brian Houghton Hodgson,* by W. W. Hunter. (London: John Murray, 1896), 249.

AILURUS, *ochraceus.*

T. Black Asiatic Lith.' Prefs Cal.

Underlying Hodgson's observations and drawings is a fondness for his wahs:

> Their manners are staid and tranquil; their movements slow and deliberate; their tempers placid and docile. . . . The amenity of their ordinary disposition is finely portrayed in their gentle countenances . . . they would make nice pets for ladies, particularly when young.

The London Zoo's Panda

In the spring of 1869, several red panda entries appear in the *Proceedings of the Zoological Society, London.* The first quotes a letter from Dr. J. Anderson, who had three wahs that he intended to ship from Calcutta to London in the company of a Dr. Simpson:

> I have a man attending them all day; and when the sun goes down I have them carried out into a cool breezy spot. . . . [T]hey are most interesting animals . . . wonderfully like Raccoons. . . . [T]hey sit up on their hindquarters and strike with

their paws in the same way as the Bear, climb like the Bear, and when irritated make the sudden rush of that animal and emit a nearly similar cry. . . . It will be a splendid success if they reach Europe alive.

The second entry in the *Proceedings* announces the arrival of a panda at the London Zoo. Percival L. Sclater, secretary, "called the attention of the Meetings to the following noticeable additions to the Society's Menagerie during the month of May." Item 5 was:

An example of the Panda *(Ailurus fulgens),* presented by Dr. H. Simpson, May 22nd, being one of three specimens obtained in the neighborhood of Darjeeling. . . . Two of the animals of this species, with which Dr. Simpson had started from Calcutta, had unfortunately died upon the voyage; the third had reached the Gardens in a very exhausted state. . . .

A WOODCUT BY JOSEPH SMIT

The first lifelike depiction of the wah accompanies the second entry. It is a woodcut by the Dutch-born animal artist Joseph Smit (1836–1929). The panda is caught in mid-stride. Its left forepaw is raised, tentatively, as it peers at the viewer. Nearby is a clump of bamboo. Smit erred in giving the panda a dark nose stripe, like that of a raccoon, a marking the white-faced panda never has. Even so, Smit's woodcut is well observed.

A third note in the 1869 *Proceedings* is by Dr. Simpson, who traveled with the panda. In addition to observations about the animal's range, its captive feeding habits, and the sounds he has heard it make, Dr. Simpson mentions having seen native people wearing panda-skin caps.

A LITHOGRAPH BY JOSEF WOLF

Plate XLI, which appears with Dr. Simpson's note on *Ailurus fulgens,* is a lithograph, also by Smit, done from a life drawing by Josef Wolf. Wolf did almost all the illustrations for the Zoological

Society's publications and was regarded as the finest animal artist of his time. He maintained that the "expression of life" was the most important thing in animal art, and he believed that the *ears,* more than an animal's eyes or the position of its head and body, conveyed expression. Wolf must have delighted in the wah's large, fluffily furred ears. His wah, the London Zoo panda, is both accurate and alive. Wolf suggests its Himalayan habitat. A red-berried sprig is clutched in the left forepaw and bamboo grows behind the boulder. Higher up among the rocks is another wah.

A. D. BARTLETT, PANDA KEEPER

As far back as he could recall, Abraham Dee Bartlett had been involved with animals. His father, a barber in London, often left his small son with a friend who was a well-known animal dealer, Mr. Edward Cross, at the Exeter Change in the Strand. As Bartlett later wrote, he was allowed "to play with young lions and other animals that were not likely to harm me." Sometimes there were giraffes and zebras at Mr. Cross's, all destined for zoos or private collections on great estates.

When he was fourteen, young Bartlett had to learn a useful trade. His father insisted he work in the barbershop. The boy was miserable. He left to study taxidermy. Skilled at skinning and mounting animals though he became, he always longed to work with *live* animals. In 1859 the London Zoo offered Bartlett the position of superintendent and with it he was given a house in Regent's Park, on the zoo grounds.

The various zoo houses had special keepers. As superintendent, Bartlett was in charge of feeding programs and the care of sick and injured animals. Often on his rounds, he would pause to talk about his animals, for he believed the zoo should be a place for learning, not just entertainment. Bearded and wearing a tall black top hat and a frock coat with flowing tails, Papa Bartlett was a popular public figure. But he was committed to his animals, so much so that his advice on animal care was sought by Queen Victoria whenever one of her numerous pets was ailing.

*Josef Wolf's portrait
of Bartlett*

On May 22, 1869, Bartlett took charge of a red panda, the first wah to reach Europe alive. It was a male, the only survivor of the three pandas that traveled by ship from Calcutta.

Barely alive, suffering from diarrhea, his fur soiled and matted, the wah had come into good hands. Bartlett discarded the feeding instructions attached to the crate: a daily ration of a quart of milk, boiled rice, and grass. He took the panda home with him. His "first object was to endeavor to support the little life that remained by a change of food."

First Bartlett tried raw and boiled chicken and some rabbit. The panda refused to eat. Then he offered egg yolks stirred with boiled milk and sugar. The panda liked this and lapped eagerly. Beef tea, also sweetened, with some pea flour and corn flour added to make a gruel, was next offered. When meat was sweetened with sugar, it too was eaten. In no time the little animal was gaining strength.

Soon Bartlett had the panda out of its cage. "Having a boy to see that he did not escape," Bartlett allowed the panda to explore his garden. It sampled leaves and rose shoots, ate some green apples on the ground. Then the panda found berry bushes. Bartlett held out a sprig with yellow berries. The panda took these, grasping "the bunch in his paw, holding it tightly, and [bit] off these berries one by one; so delighted with this food was he that all other food was left as long as these berries lasted." He noted that the "thickly muffled," fur-covered paws "would lead one to doubt whether the panda could grasp with its paw as firmly and perfectly as I have seen it do." And he concluded that "berries, fruit, and other vegetable substances" are the panda's diet in the wild.

Bartlett recognized the panda's efforts to clean its worn, ragged coat: "Animals recovering from sickness show signs of improvement by their attempts to clean themselves." So, on sunny mornings he sprinkled the wah with a garden sprayer before letting him out of the cage. The wah shook vigorously, then bit and scratched to rid himself of old fur. After that, he settled himself to bask in the warm sunshine.

Obviously the panda was recovering. New fur, red and black, was growing in. But Bartlett found the wah unpredictable. Sometimes it rushed at him like a bear, forelimbs raised to strike. Sharp spitting hisses and squeak calls accompanied these threats. For all Mr. Bartlett's devoted care, the animal remained a "fierce little panda."

As a zoo man, Bartlett felt that the panda was most like the kinkajou, a furry, fruit-eating member of the raccoon family. Both animals grasp plant stems and fruits in their forepaws, and both run through the trees or over the ground "jumping with a kind of gallop." Bartlett added that he believed the kinkajou, with its prehensile tail, to be the more agile climber and to have "a far higher intelligence."

Bartlett took note of the wah's other **procyonid** features: fur that was somewhat like that of the coati, forepaw dexterity that reminded him of the raccoon. But the panda, he pointed out, was "slower in all its movements" than kinkajou, coati, or raccoon.

coatis

kinkajou

raccoon

SIR WILLIAM H. FLOWER, ANATOMIST

On December 12, 1869, the London Zoo panda died. Bartlett was grieved and wanted to determine the cause of its death. He sent the body to the Royal College of Surgeons for examination by Professor William H. Flower.

Except for a few lesions in the intestines and the "soft and spongy" nature of the bones, a condition he had previously observed in captive animals, the anatomist found the nine-and-a-half-pound panda to be in "exceedingly good condition."

Flower looked carefully at the panda's furred feet and curved claws. He peered into its mouth and commented that the *rugae* were low. These are the folds on the roof of the mouth that increase the area for evaporative cooling when an animal pants. Just behind the upper incisor teeth he found a small but conspicuous hollow. The tongue, thick and fleshy at the back, was flattened in front and it had little extension. The panda's teeth, Flower decided, were "essentially formed upon the same plan as those of *Procyon*" (the raccoon).

In spite of the raccoon affinities he saw, Flower remained uncertain as to whether the wah should be grouped with the raccoon and its relatives or kept in a family of its own. Perhaps, he thought, the determination could be delayed until more was known about the "remarkable new mammal lately obtained in Eastern Tibet, a creature as large as some of the smaller species of Bear" that also had raccoonlike teeth.

Flower was troubled by the fact that other carnivore families, such as the **ursids** (bears) and the **mustelids** (weasels and badgers), are found in both the Old World and the New World while raccoons and their relatives were thought to be strictly New World mammals.

Pandas of the Past

The fossil record indicates that the wah's ancestors did have a wide distribution. *Parailurus,* an extinct wahlike mammal, was discovered in 1899. Fragments of its skulls and teeth have been recovered from Pliocene rocks, two million to seven million years old, in central and southern Europe.

One species of this panda progenitor lived in North America. In 1977 Richard D. Tedford, of the American Museum of Natural History, and E. P. Gustafson, of the University of Texas, reported on the finding of a right upper first molar tooth from stream-deposited sediments of Pliocene age near Yakima, Washington. Unlike the wider-than-long molars of living wahs and the nearly square molars of the robust *Parailurus* of Europe, this *Parailurus* tooth is intermediate in size and slightly longer than wide. So, it is clear that long ago the red panda's ancestors inhabited temperate forests that stretched across much of the northern parts of the Old and the New Worlds.

As the Pleistocene glaciations caused retreat of the temperate forests, small isolated stretches of forest were left behind in what is now southwestern China. In these relict forest communities the red panda *(Ailurus),* smaller in size and its range much reduced, survived. Fossil wahs, much like the living red panda, have been found in mid-Pleistocene rocks in Yunnan Province.

Other animals survived with the wah—the giant panda and the beautiful orange-furred golden monkey, a diminutive deer called the muntjac, and the goatlike serow.

The continuing uplift of the Himalaya during Pleistocene time caused moister conditions to prevail. Eventually new mountain-forest habitat developed and the wah slowly extended its range westward into the Himalayan region.

The Other Panda

For centuries the Chinese had known of a large white-and-black animal they called *beishung* (white bear), but it was not until 1869, when Père David sent word to Alphonse Milne-Edwards in Paris of "a remarkable bear" he had collected, that the giant panda was "discovered." After careful examination of the panda skulls sent by Père David, Milne-Edwards was convinced the animal had close affinities to the raccoon and the small panda.

As other giant panda specimens came under scrutiny, scientists began to argue. Some, after comparing braincase characters, claimed the giant panda was an unusual bear. Others said it was a member of the raccoon family. Often they failed to consider panda features that did not fit the theory they promoted. The wah, being the original panda, was much involved in the controversy. One authority, British zoologist R. I. Pocock, decided that neither panda belonged with the raccoon group and proposed that each be placed in its own family.

How closely related are giant and red pandas? And how closely related are the two pandas either to raccoons or to bears? Even today, scientists quibble about where in the taxonomic scheme of things the two pandas belong.

The red panda is in many ways raccoonlike, while the giant panda is bearlike. Yet the skulls of the two pandas, as well as their tooth structure, are remarkably similar. And, for all its raccoon resemblance in body size and ringed tail, the red panda—if changed from red to white and given a short tail—comes close to being a small version of the giant panda.

After years of work on the anatomy of the giant panda in his laboratory at the Field Museum of Natural History in Chicago, D. Dwight Davis came to the conclusion that "every morphological feature . . . indicates the giant panda is nothing more than a highly specialized bear. . . ." He went on to note that the red panda had a remarkably similar masticatory apparatus for chewing bamboo, and a similar forepaw specialization for manipulating bamboo stems.

Such similarities in form and function may have evolved in both pandas during isolation in their mountain-forest environment. While the red panda has continued to feed largely on bamboo leaves, the big panda added stems to its diet. Its bear size may be a bodily **adaptation** to consuming this tougher plant material.

As for the wah's raccoonlike characteristics, no one knows for certain whether they are primitive features of a separate family, or features that have been acquired through time and are **convergent.** Convergence is the development of similar characteristics, behavioral as well as structural, in animals that are not closely related.

Ecological factors, the variables of habitat and climate, affect an animal's behavior. Feeding strategy depends on food availability and influences the pattern of activity and social organization. Thus, two animals such as red panda and giant panda, occupying similar habitats, may have developed through time similar behavior patterns without being closely related.

Evolutionary trees can be constructed on the basis of various kinds of scientific evidence. On some trees all three groups (pandas, raccoons, bears) occupy two separate stems, descending from a common carnivore ancestor that lived 30 million to 50 million years ago. The raccoon stem divides early. One branch leads to the red panda, the other has twigs for ringtail, raccoon, coati, kinkajou, and olingo (all members of the raccoon family). Later in geologic time the bear stem splits. A single branch leads to the giant panda. The other supports twigs for the various bears.

Not all scientists acknowledge a bear or raccoon grouping of the pandas. Dedicated red-panda researchers Miles Roberts, of the National Zoological Park, and John Gittleman, of the University of Tennessee, admit their animal does show raccoon similarities. But they maintain that the ecological and feeding specializations of the red panda indicate it is better placed by itself in the Ailuridae, a family derived from the raccoon group.

While blood protein studies by Vincent Sarich, of the University of California at Berkeley, imply the red panda is an early offshoot of the giant panda and bears line, molecular analyses by Stephen J. O'Brien and his colleagues at the National Cancer Institute group the red panda with the raccoon and its relatives.

At the National Museum of Natural History, W. Chris Wozencraft points out that it is only mammalogists in North America who regard the wah as a member of the raccoon family. He cites the similarities of the procyonids to some European animals, all belonging to an Old World carnivore family, the **viverrids.** These look-alike pairs, exhibiting comparable ecological needs and behavioristic traits, include ringtail and genet, coati and mongoose, raccoon and civet.

Wozencraft's comparative study of some 100 characters of teeth, skull, skeleton, and soft anatomy leads him to believe the red panda belongs with the bears. He places the wah on the first twig on the branch of the bear family, and he prefers that the red panda be called the tree bear and the giant panda be called the bamboo bear.

Where Panda Ranges Overlap

Arthur de Carle Sowerby, founder and curator of the Shanghai Natural History Museum, was an authority on China and its animals. His wanderings took him into the craggy mountains and deeply dissected ravines of Sichuan Province, the haunt of both red panda and giant panda.

Sowerby apparently had a firsthand acquaintance with the wah, finding it a "delightful little creature, which becomes very tame in captivity and is exceedingly playful." He also was an artist, the son, grandson, and great-grandson of Sowerbys, all noted illustrators of natural history subjects. In a watercolor painted in the late 1800s he depicts the two pandas in a forest of blossoming rhododendrons. Their gnarled and twisted stems are draped with beards of lichens. Primulas grow on moss-covered rocks. A thicket of bamboo is food for both the pandas.

2

Red Pandas Today

The Wah in Wolong

Wolong Natural Reserve is one of twelve reserves in Sichuan Province set aside by the Chinese government to protect the dwindling habitat of the giant panda. It is also a center for giant-panda research.

When George Schaller, of the New York Zoological Society, began his three-year study of the giant pandas of Wolong, he found that red pandas also lived in the reserve. The wahs themselves were rarely glimpsed, but their tracks, droppings, resting places, and feeding signs were evident.

One night in February 1984 a female red panda wandered into one of the giant panda traps. The surprised researchers, Schaller and his colleagues Kenneth Johnson, of the University of Tennessee, and Hu Jinchu, of Nanchong Normal College, had their first close look at a wild-caught red panda. They decided to call her Jiao. Around her neck they carefully fitted a radio transmitter collar.

Radio tracking is used to study the ways of animals that are nocturnal and live in dense cover. As the team maintained daily contact

19

with five radio-collared giant pandas, they also began to collect the first radio-telemetry data on a wah. For nine months Jiao's resting places were plotted and her times of activity were monitored.

Each wah has its own **home range**, the area over which it roams in the course of its normal activities. Within the seasonally shifting boundaries of a home range are core areas of intensive use. Jiao's home range, an area of some three square kilometers (about two square miles), was almost completely overlapped by the twice-as-large home range of one of the giant pandas, Wei. When Jiao and Wei were attracted to a flourishing patch of bamboo, they sometimes foraged within a hundred meters (just over three hundred feet) of each other.

Jiao's activity pattern showed little variation from month to month or from day to day. She stirred at dusk and was active through the night with short periods of rest. Before dawn her activity peaked. During the day she rested for two long periods of time, sometimes on a fallen log, on or in a stump, or at the base of a large tree.

A Field Study in Nepal

In the Cholang-Dokache area of Nepal a red panda project is under way, supported by the World Wildlife Fund and the King Mahendra Trust for Nature Conservation. It took Pralad Yonzon 787 man-hours of looking to locate five wahs. At least five but perhaps as many as eight pandas live within the nineteen square kilometers (nearly twelve square miles) of his study area.

Capturing a wah is not easy. When live traps baited with biscuits and jam failed to attract the wahs, Yonzon turned to a search-and-capture method. Once located high in a tree or pursued over the ground to a tree trunk, a panda was noosed. Yonzon and his helpers then eased the struggling animal into a cloth bag so that it could be weighed. Through the bag an intramuscular injection of ketamine hydrochloride (8.8 mm/kg of body weight) was given. Within minutes eyelids blinked, then body muscles relaxed. Once the wah was immobilized Yonzon and his team could examine it, determine the sex, put on an ear tag, and then fit around its neck a small, battery-powered radio transmitter with a wire whip antenna. For a twenty-four-hour period the released panda was carefully watched.

Three wahs were radio-collared in the first months of the study, a male marked as 101 and two females, 102 and 103. Each panda's transmitter broadcasts at an individual frequency. For five days every month the team monitored each of the pandas. As he climbed about the steep slopes, Pralad Yonzon carried a receiver and antenna. He determined a wah's location by intensity of the beeps from its collar transmitter. He took care never to upset the wahs by approaching too close. By plotting fixes on a map and connecting the outer points, each animal's home range was outlined. Continual recording of their radio signals revealed daily activity patterns.

Home-range estimates were smaller than those plotted for Jiao. Females 102 and 103 had home ranges of .48 and .60 square kilometers (.29 and .37 square miles). Although there appeared to be no overlap of the areas they frequented, wahs, at least the females, probably do have overlapping home ranges. The male, a young ani-

mal, was monitored at **dispersal** time, when he was leaving the area where he was born. He moved north from the study area to occupy a .73 square-kilometer (.45 square-mile) home range.

As field work goes on, Pralad Yonzon hopes to learn more about the wah's habitat preferences, find out the areas it uses most within its home ranges, and determine the shift of home-range boundaries as different foods become available during the year.

Predators and People

Occasionally in winter a snow leopard follows deer and sheep down-slope into the forest home of the wah. The cat's long, thick coat is a soft gray, marked by brown blotches, each ringed in black. Its long, heavily furred tail is nearly as long as its body. On furred feet that are like snowshoes it pads over the snow, usually in early morning or late in the afternoon. A snow leopard's territory is large, so large it may

take a week or so to traverse. An unwary wah might be the victim of this stalk-and-spring hunter, but the snow leopard's usual prey includes marmots, birds, deer, and sheep.

Another occasional visitor is the clouded leopard. Black stripes, spots, and blotches mark the coat of this stout-limbed cat that rests and does much of its hunting in trees and kills with a swat of a broad forepaw.

A wah cub may be snatched by a **raptor,** an owl that swoops on silent wings in the night, or a hawk that drops into a tree in the daytime.

The wah's real enemies are man and his dogs. Pandas once were hunted for their skins. Caps that look much like the Daniel Boone coonskin caps of the American frontier were fashioned. As many as thirty skins were needed to make a rug. Tails were used for brushes and dusters. Even today, trapping takes a toll. Sometimes a wah is caught in a snare set for musk deer.

Pralad Yonzon's field-study area in Nepal was invaded during the summer by 500 cows. With them came yaks, herdsmen, and some forty-five mastiff dogs. Free to roam at night, the dogs killed at least two wah cubs.

The red panda's range, once an arc that extended westward from the Chinese provinces of Yunnan and Sichuan across southeastern Tibet and northern Burma, through Bhutan and Sikkim into Nepal, is diminished. Wahs are gone from Sikkim. In Nepal and in China, wahs, like so many other animals around the world, compete for living space with ever-increasing human populations.

Panda habitat is destroyed as forests are cut down and agriculture and grazing push up mountain slopes. Deforestation affects the soil's capacity for holding water. Streams dry up, then flow violently when it rains or when snow melts. These conditions are unfavorable for the growth of bamboo, the staple of the wah's diet. Stretches of forest that once were vast are reduced to mountain-slope patches connected

A village in Nepal

by forested ridges. As Miles Roberts notes, the wah is squeezed "into smaller and smaller areas capable of supporting fewer and fewer animals."

This increasing isolation of small populations endangers the wah. Unless wahs can move freely by way of forested corridors, small isolated groups are subject to starvation if food sources are depleted. Diseases and parasites are more easily transmitted from animal to animal. And there is danger of **inbreeding** leading to a lack of **genetic variability** that is itself a weakness. Then the death rate for cubs increases and the animals are even more vulnerable to diseases and parasite infestations.

The wah is protected in India, Bhutan, Nepal, and China, and its listing by CITES (Convention on the International Trade in Threatened and Endangered Species) restricts animal dealers in exporting wahs caught in the wild.

As a buffer against the time when even remnant areas of forest are threatened, breeding programs such as the one at the National Zoo in Washington, D.C., and its Conservation and Research Center in Front Royal, Virginia, are essential to insure there always will be wahs.

Around the world some fifty-two zoos that have red pandas share information on care, feeding, cub development, and troubles that afflict their wahs. At the Rotterdam Zoo an international studbook is maintained, which lists all the pandas in captivity.

Efforts are being made to preserve habitat for the wah and other rare animals. The World Wildlife Fund established the Annapurna Conservation Area in Nepal, a sanctuary for wahs, snow leopards, and other rare animals. The area includes a deep valley—the Kali Gandaki—and some of the highest mountains in the world. More importantly for wahs, there are lush forests of rhododendron and bamboo-covered slopes.

Wolong is the largest of China's giant panda preserves, where wahs also have protection, but even in reserves people have their impact on the environment.

The Wah at Home

Temperate forests of the Himalaya and the high mountains of northern Burma and western China, at elevations of 2,200 to 4,800 meters (7,218 to 15,749 feet), are red panda habitat.

Cool and wet weather prevails in panda country, especially during summer. The rainy season lasts from June through October. Most of the rainfall occurs at night. In daytime fog shrouds the lower slopes. Spruce and fir boughs sag with moisture. Everywhere water trickles and drips. All this summertime wetness causes bamboos to sprout and later on results in an abundance of mushrooms and other fungi that by early fall dot the forest floor.

By frosty November the **deciduous** trees have lost most of their colorful leaves. When winter comes, with cold and snow, rhododendron leaves curl tightly and bamboo becomes rigid. Ice glazes the

rocks in streams. Snow burdens evergreen branches and bends bamboo fronds. Still there is green, because **coniferous** trees, rhododendrons, and bamboo keep their green leaves. Where snow has melted, the green of mosses and ferns is exposed. And there are days, even weeks, when the high peaks stand sharp-edged against a brilliant blue sky.

March marks the end of winter. Snows that fall at night disappear in daytime warmth. By April rhododendrons begin to flower. Ferns push up through the leaf litter. Buds of larches, birch, and maple show soft greens.

In the Himalaya of Nepal, rounded mountains with steep valley slopes and streams are backed by a virtual wall of sharp-peaked mountains, the highest peaks in the world. Rivers that flow southward from the Tibetan plateau dissect this vast mountain chain, cutting deep north-south gorges. Differences in temperature and rainfall create climatic zones that stack one atop the other, each with its associated animals and plants.

Miles Roberts describes a climb through terraced fields of rice and barley, through yak pastures, and up into the Tiru Dara range:

> Our trail dipped through small canyons and gullies that were washed by streams from the slowly melting snow and ice of the distant mountains. Bamboo lined the permanent bodies of water . . . as we climbed ridge after ridge, the rhododendron forest gave way to mixed stands of hemlock, spruce, and yew, then to larch and fir. . . .

In Nepal, typical panda habitat is a mixed forest of firs and hemlocks, chestnuts, oaks, and maples. It is the haunt of one of the two subspecies of the red panda, the Himalayan or Western Red Panda, *Ailurus fulgens fulgens*.

Wahs are rarely seen in Nepal. Miles Roberts counts himself fortunate. During a month and a half in the field he glimpsed two pandas and admits: "If they hadn't been moving, I never would have seen them." Sleeping high up in fir trees festooned with red moss clumps

and beards of white lichens, the pandas were concealed until they stirred. Quickly they climbed down and scurried off through the underbrush.

In the eastern part of its range, in Bhutan and along the Burma-Yunnan border, the wah is more frequently spotted, but even there its numbers are few.

The mountains of western China trend north to south and trap wind-driven, moisture-laden clouds deep in their shadowed canyons. Beech and hemlock grow on steep slopes broken by cliffs. On lower slopes rhododendrons and other shrubs flourish. Thorny plants grow along trails and in open glades. Wherever the forest floor is moist and well drained, the growth of bamboo is fostered.

Pandas in the Yunnan-Sichuan highlands are larger and their fur is a more intense rust color. They belong to the subspecies *Ailurus fulgens styani,* Styan's red panda, described in 1902 by British Museum scientist Oldfield Thomas and named in honor of F. W. Styan, donor of a large collection of mammals from China.

There are other animals in the wah's bamboo-forest home. Beneath the thickets stout-bodied, short-legged bamboo rats excavate their burrows. They feed underground, using their large, orange incisor teeth to cut bamboo roots. At night they emerge to feed on above-ground parts of bamboo. During the day golden monkeys, with long, silky, orange manes and bright blue noses, come to feed on bamboo leaves. Occasionally an Asian black bear, a white moon on its chest, forages on the slopes.

The shaggy-coated takin, a close relative of the North American musk-ox, climbs on steep cliffs and rests and browses in bamboo thickets. Another of the goat-antelopes, the serow, uses its short, sharp horns to defend its small mountain-slope feeding area.

At Home in the Zoo

More and more, zoos are creating zoogeographic exhibits with landscaped enclosures and invisible fencing. Often you must look and look before you spot the animals. This is the way animals are seen in the wild. The reward is seeing an animal "doing its thing"—foraging, exploring, playing, sometimes just resting or sleeping.

The Himalayan Highlands at the New York Zoological Park (Bronx Zoo) is a two-and-a-half-acre exhibit that simulates mountainous terrain in Nepal and Tibet. This small world of rocky cliffs, rhododendron thickets, conifer stands, and a rushing stream is home to snow leopards and to red pandas.

But it is the wahs that attract zoo visitors. Li Ning and Tong Fei, young males acquired from the Knoxville Zoo's breeding program, find much to do in their forest habitat. There are trees to climb, logs, stumps, and rocks to deposit scent on, a small stream to drink from, and best of all, bamboo to eat.

Stand quietly on the deck and watch. Tong Fei is draped on a branch almost within reach. Li Ning has gone down to explore the forest floor, trotting bowlegged beneath the rhododendrons and laurel. "What *are* they?" asks one visitor. "Oh, they're so beautiful." "It's not a fox, it's a *red* panda." Whatever they are doing when people come to see them, Li Ning and Tong Fei delight their visitors.

3

The Ways of Wahs

Communication Among Wahs

Although red pandas tolerate the company of their own kind in zoos where they are exhibited in pairs or family groups and are often seen feeding together or resting in the branches of a single tree, in the wild wahs live apart. But even so-called solitary animals communicate. They exchange information by means of smells and sounds, as well as by visual signals.

A PANDA'S PLACE

Wahs establish **scat stations,** places where they defecate. In captivity their scat stations usually are located along the periphery of the enclosure. In the wild their **scats** are deposited at the base of trees or along trails. Because a wah stays in the same area for days, its scat stations tend to be clustered. George Schaller describes a winter site "much used by red pandas" where, in addition to scattered feces, there were a number of large piles where wahs had defecated again and again. Near the most-used scat station was a conspicuous ground hollow, presumably excavated by a panda as a resting place. Paw-

packed snow trails in the area were marked by urine sprinkles, as were snow-covered logs.

Paired anal glands, found in dissection to contain a pungent greenish black oily fluid, connect by short ducts to the rectum and presumably add scent significance to a scat station.

When investigating the scat station of an unknown animal, a wah sniffs carefully, then gives a vigorous head shake before continuing on its way.

SCENT POSTS

Wahs are scent markers. A clear fluid, secreted by glands around the anus, is combined with urine and used for posting scent. This **pheromone,** or chemical signal used in communication, is a sticky secretion that transmits in darkness and lasts for days.

Communication depends upon scent marking and sampling. Scent posts are carefully chosen environmental objects, such as the end of a hollow log, a root, the edge of a boulder, the edge of a den-box entrance, places where globs of the glandular secretion accumulate. First sampled by sniffing, a scent post often is updated by the investigator.

The ritualized behavior of scent marking helps pandas avoid one another. Scent marking also reveals when and where individuals travel and enables a wah to maintain contact and recognize its neighbors, other wahs it may encounter occasionally.

Excitement triggers frequent quick waddles in which the anal region is pressed against an object with one or more rotating motions of the wah's hind end. This kind of scent marking occurs when an animal is released in a new enclosure, or when a new keeper takes over panda care, or when a cluster of visitors or loud noises stress a wah.

A wah posts scent

But most of the time a panda scent-marks to reassure itself within its own area and to post information for other wahs.

A panda uses specialized motor patterns to post scent. Each of the several ways of marking conveys particular kinds of information.

The male sniffs a scent post, straddles it, crouches, or sometimes cocks a hind leg, and then rubs side to side. He urinates, rubs back and forth with his lower belly on the object. Then with his anal region he makes circular movements to deposit scent-gland secretion.

The female also sniffs, then straddles a scent post. She uses circular and side-to-side rubs of her lowered rump and up-and-down jerks of her tail to deposit scent. The male-female difference in marking techniques probably reveals information on sex and reproductive condition.

A scent post may be passed without inspection, briefly sniffed, or carefully examined. Scent is vapor. Inhaled and warmed as it passes through the nasal passages, it can provide detailed messages. When an odor is difficult to assess by sniffing, a wah tongue-tests, or tastes by applying the undersurface of its tongue tip to the marked object.

Observing this behavior, Miles Roberts took a look at a wah's tongue. In a small median groove on the underside, near the tip, he found a cluster of tiny fleshy projections that may have a gustatory, or tasting, function.

The small pit in the wah's mouth, noticed by Sir William Flower when he dissected the London Zoo panda, is the **vomeronasal** (or Jacobson's) **organ.** It too may function in smell-taste discrimination. Located just behind the upper incisor teeth, it is lined with receptor cells and connects by a small duct to the nasal passages. From it, nerve fibers trace to the hypothalamus, the pea-sized center of the brain that correlates information from the animal's surroundings.

Occasionally a wah is seen to sniff and then exhibit a slight open-mouth pant. While this facial gesture is not the lips-drawn-up grimace, the **flehmen,** of some other carnivores, it may well direct inhaled vapor into the vomeronasal pit for more detailed olfactory analysis.

SCENT TRAILS

A wah's home range includes tree trails as well as ground routes. Body rubs mark small branches and twigs. Much like a cat, the panda pushes forward, pressing its neck and shoulder against the object.

On tree branches the panda lays a trail of scent. Between the furred pads of the paws, Miles Roberts found a series of small pores, each marked by a few longer and coarser hairs. The colorless fluid secreted by these modified sweat glands forms a trail of scent that helps to familiarize a wah with its home range and enables it to get about at night. Scent trails are continuous and readily followed as the wah now and again drops its head to sniff. The branches of a tree that is much used by a wah will be coated with the sticky secretion.

WAH CALLS

Although they can be vocal, wahs are silent most of the time. Miles Roberts found seven distinct calls.

A small cub's whistle call, *wheee* or *wheeet,* signals distress and brings its mother to the den. Quack-snorts, *hhhhk-hk-hk-hk,* are used in threat situations, often when a wah, with open mouth and raised forepaws, strikes an opponent. A high-pitched twitter is a contact call, *we-ee-ee-oo,* heard only during breeding season and more often from males than from females. Twice Roberts heard males bleat, a sound similar to the bleat of the giant panda.

The wah has an explosive exhalant *whuufff,* much like that of the raccoon. When there is den disturbance, even small cubs emit warning *whuufff*s, at the same time violently humping their bodies to frighten off the intruder. When a wah is attacked it squeals *weeeeee.* And in the scuffle that ensues, grunts *unhh, unhh* accompany its efforts to wriggle free.

Mammals that rely on their sense of hearing to locate prey or detect predators tend to have enlarged **auditory bullae,** bony chambers that enclose the middle ear and provide for increased sensitivity to sounds. The small size of these paired capsules on the base of a wah's skull suggests that hearing is not the animal's most important sense.

Because it spends so much time in trees where the noise of wind-tossed branches, rattling leaves, and sometimes the pattering of rain obscure other sounds, a wah depends more on a well-developed sense of smell and on sight.

When Wahs Meet

Wahs in the wild keep their distance through a system of mutual avoidance. Except during mating season, encounters are infrequent. Neighbors, pandas with adjacent home ranges, are recognized. At night, in whatever light there is, the whitish face may be the only part of a wah that is visible. Tear tracks and forehead patterns, differing in shape and definition (degree of darkness), are individual. Although related animals may have similar markings, no two wahs are exactly alike. It may be that wahs recognize one another's faces at a distance.

From a tree limb the resident panda, ears forward and head extended, stares intently at a wah interloper. Actual meeting involves inspection. The pandas nose-dab, as one tests the other. Their sniffing extends to their necks. Then, with a quack-snort, the wah takes a deliberate forepaw swat at the newcomer.

Passing on a branch, pandas make quick, darting motions to sniff at each other's sides. From the rear one turns to sniff the other's flank. Often a male checks by pushing his muzzle beneath another wah's tail.

In all the carnivores, face and ears reveal emotion and emphasize expression, so it is not surprising that a number of them, like the wah, have masks or tear tracks and ears that are heavily furred, tufted, or conspicuously patterned. Aggression is rare among wahs. An **agnostic** (unfriendly) **encounter,** when it occurs, is marked by visual displays and vocal accompaniment.

When a wah, kept for a time in an adjacent enclosure, is released in an occupied yard, it scent-marks and explores and scent-marks again. As another wah approaches there is defensive posturing by both animals. Tails and backs are arched. They turn their heads and jaw-clap. Head bobbing occurs and low warning *whuufff*s sound. A forepaw is raised, as though to swat.

The ultimate threat display is the **bipedal** (two-footed) strike. The wah stands tall, its forelimbs upstretched so that the paws are at ear level. Huff-quacks announce intent. Its tail is a furry prop. Then, mouth open, the wah lunges, striking with its forelimbs.

If a fight ensues, there is squealing from the attacked panda. Grunts and snorts punctuate the tussle as furry forms tangle, rolling and tumbling, clinging, grappling, and ripping with hind feet, and biting. Bites are directed at the heavily furred cheeks and ears, shoulders, flanks, and base of tail.

More often, as Miles Roberts has seen, wahs settle "into patterns of mutual tolerance through avoidance." They establish their own resting and sleeping places and maintain "discrete spacing between one another when moving about the enclosure."

Times of Activity

Wahs are **crepuscular** (active at twilight and daybreak) and **nocturnal** (active at night). During the night there are short periods of activity and times of rest.

Field data from the radio-collared pandas in Nepal reveal three nighttime peaks of activity during summer. Wahs are active at night between 10:30 and 11:30 P.M., between 12:30 and 1:30 A.M., and from 2:30 to 3:30 A.M. Daytime activity occurs between 5:30 and 7:30 A.M., between 2 and 4 P.M., and from 7:30 to 8:30 P.M. Resting or sleeping periods range from fifteen minutes to five hours. In all, a wah is awake and stirring from ten to fourteen hours out of twenty-four.

Radio-tracking data on the Wolong wah indicate a very nocturnal way of life, but this is influenced by weather, time of year, the dependence of cubs in the den, and predators that may be in the area. Where there is persecution by people and dogs, wahs, like raccoons, restrict their activity to the dark of night.

Zoo pandas, many of them born in captivity, adapt to different schedules. Li Ning and Tong Fei, the wahs at the Bronx Zoo, are fed in their indoor quarters in late afternoon and confined for the night, so during the day they often are active.

At the National Zoo fresh bamboo branches and food trays of gruel* and slices of apple and banana are set out in the morning. Then zoo visitors who come by about feeding time see red pandas in motion.

As Keeper Steve Clevenger and his assistant Amy Van Houten approach, the pandas peer down with interest. Bamboo is placed near the pool, the two food pans set down near the big den box at the base of the mulberry tree.

Then comes daily cleanup. Stripped bamboo stalks are removed and the pool is cleared of leafy debris. The keeper knows scat station locations and moves quickly from one to another for pickup with rake and pan.

---

*Gruel for wahs is made of oatmeal baby cereal mixed with evaporated milk, applesauce, honey, and a vitamin supplement.

Soon after Steve and Amy leave the enclosure, the female, whose name is Eunice, moves up higher on the mulberry branch where she has been resting. She grooms: one hind foot, then the other, then her tail. Herb leaves his favorite tree fork in the mulberry and moves out

along a branch. Eunice continues to groom, scratching her chin and throat with a forepaw. With right hind foot she scratches her cheek and ear, then uses her left hind foot to work on her shoulder. She shakes, moves down the limb and down the trunk. At the main fork she crosses over and goes up the other side of the tree.

Herb comes directly down the trunk, headfirst. He enters the den box, turns, comes out, and feeds for several minutes on gruel. He strides across the enclosure and along the near rim of the pool, just in front of excited zoo visitors. He pauses in the north corner to urinate, then trots along the far rim of the pool, heads for the mulberry, and climbs up.

Some ten minutes later Eunice comes down. She shows no interest in the food trays. Or the bamboo branches. She moves along the far side of the pool. Even her white-furred paw pads are reflected in the water. She investigates the scat station, then reverses her route. She stops at the big rock, defecates, then trots to the mulberry. Her white-fringed, black-backed ears are conspicuous as she disappears through the tall grass.

Once back in the tree, Eunice appears agitated. Keepers are cleaning in the nearby bear dens. And she has two small cubs in the nursery den below. On this late July day, as the sun moves overhead, it is hot. Herb drapes on a favorite branch. Eunice, agitated and feeling the heat, pants.

Miles Roberts conducted four twenty-four-hour watches—winter, spring, summer, and fall—in the pandas' enclosure. He found there are seasonal shifts in their activity pattern.

Beginning several hours after dark, the wintertime pattern shows three peaks of activity and ends at sunrise. By May, the female, now pregnant, comes down from the mulberry tree for a midday drink. Night activity starts three hours before dark and has two peaks. And both pandas are still active at sunrise.

In July there are cubs in the nursery den. Activity peaks lengthen as the female spends longer times feeding. On very hot days the pair rests in the tree and does not stir until after dark.

By September the cubs begin to leave the den on their own, in the daytime as well as at night. Three daytime peaks of activity record the mother's concern for her cubs. Just before sunset activity increases and continues through the night until about 4 A.M.

In the Trees and on the Ground

Because the red panda usually is seen resting or sleeping in a tree, it sometimes is referred to as an **arboreal** (tree-living) animal even though it spends much of its waking hours moving over and foraging about on the forest floor. A more accurate term for the wah is **scansorial.** It is an animal adapted for climbing.

CLIMBING

Wahs are superb climbers. Brian Houghton Hodgson claims: "As climbers no quadrupeds can surpass, and very few equal them." A

wah goes up a tree much as it moves on the ground, with a cross-extension gait of fore- and hind limbs. When there is reason, it bounds up a tree trunk.

The panda's bearlike paws are five-toed and have strongly curved pinkish-white claws that are half sheathed and partially retractile. This prevents blunting by wear when the wah travels over hard ground and rocks. Sharp claws are essential climbing tools.

Once in a tree, the wah is agile as it moves from branch to branch and up and down. Pectoral (chest) and pelvic girdles, as well as limb joints, are flexible and its spine has vertical mobility. Its limb mus-

culature is powerful. Stout forelimbs swing out in a lateral arc, a motion that accommodates its pigeon-toed forepaws to the rounded contour of a branch.

For its size, the wah is relatively light. Body weight ranges from 3.7 to 6.2 kilograms (8 to 14 pounds). This allows a wah to climb high among the thinner branches of a tree where a heavier predator cannot follow.

At the National Zoo anatomist Theodore Grand combines data from dissection with observations of live animals in comparing the musculature of two climbers: red panda and raccoon. Although the panda is the less muscular of the two animals, it is "where they put their muscle" that differs. The panda, with more muscle in its forelimbs and its tail, appears evenly muscled, while a raccoon, going up

a tree trunk or settling on its haunches to feed, is pear-shaped. Distribution of the extensor back muscles, important in climbing, accounts for this difference in body outlines. In the wah the extensors are "smeared out" along the back. In the raccoon these same muscles are concentrated in the lumbar (between ribs and pelvis) region, for propulsion in bounding over the ground and for hasty ascent.

The wah's long, heavy tail functions for balance. It flows behind the body, sometimes arched, sometimes straight, but always the graceful extension of the animal's movement. When a wah stands tall on its hind legs, its tail is a prop.

COMING DOWN

Hind feet reveal the true scansorial nature of wahs. They descend from their tree resting places sometimes slowly, sometimes rapidly, but always headfirst. Or, as Brian Hodgson notes, "without any necessity for 'turning their backs on themselves.'" Hind-foot mobility makes headfirst descent possible. Rotated outward at the ankle, a wah's hind feet are partially reversed so that its sharp, curved hind claws grasp the trunk.

In varying degrees some other animals exhibit this arboreal adaptation of swiveling their hind feet: the raccoon and its relatives, the gray squirrel, and the opossum. The ankle joint is made up of seven bones. In most mammals its movement is restricted to a fore-and-aft plane. Hind-foot rotation occurs in some swivel-footed mammals just within the ankle joint, while in others there is also slight rotation at the knee and/or hip joints.

Headfirst descent has an obvious advantage. Not only is it faster than backing down, as a cat or a bear does, but it positions a wah to hit the ground running, so that it can make a quick departure through the underbrush.

ON THE GROUND

The panda is **semiplantigrade,** flat-footed except that the heels of its hind feet rarely touch the ground. It walks, sometimes purposefully or, when foraging, slowly from place to place. Often it uses fallen logs as travel routes and for access to bamboo leaves that are high up.

When momentum is increased, a wah ambles. Then its legs on either side move almost, but not quite, as a pair. To cover ground

faster, it moves into a trot, a two-beat diagonal gait with only two feet touching the ground at a time.

When frightened a wah flees galloping, sometimes half bounding. With hind feet pushing off together, one forepaw landing and then the other, its back arched and its tail raised, it reaches the safety of a tree.

Resting and Sleeping

The wah rests and sleeps in trees, on fallen logs, or shelters at the base of a trunk or stump. Weather conditions dictate how it rests. Often it curls on its side on a branch or in the fork of a limb. Cold and rain, or snow, cause a wah to curl more tightly, drawing its black, fur-insulated limbs closer to its body. With nose tucked under a hind limb and its tail, a warm muffler, draped over paws and face, the panda sleeps.

Sometimes to keep warm or just to escape from daytime distractions, a panda draws its hind limbs under its body and rolls forward on the branch, so that its head is tucked beneath its chest, its nose pushed between its hind feet. Then it tucks in its forepaws.

Even when it is cold, wahs sleep by themselves. But a mother and cubs, or two siblings, sometimes curl together on a branch for huddled warmth.

On warm days a panda stretches out on a limb, belly pressed to the bark and legs dangling. This draped position gives the body maximum exposure to whatever breeze is stirring. To keep light out, the wah puts forepaws over its face.

The wah's coat color is **cryptic,** or concealing. A resting panda closely resembles a clump of reddish brown moss and white lichens, plants that festoon the branches of fir trees in its mountain-forest habitat. Even on the ground the panda's pattern can be concealing.

hind end. It pulls against its firmly placed hind legs, for several seconds enjoying the stretch of muscles. Sometimes a closed-eyes yawn accompanies the stretch. Then comes a head-and-body shake.

Shaking can be purposeful as well as pleasurable. In rain and snow a wah gets wet. Then a vigorous head-to-tail shake gets rid of water that accumulates on the outercoat of smooth, red guard hairs.

Drinking

A. D. Bartlett describes the panda drinking like a bear, by inserting its lips and sucking, and not by lapping. But this panda, pausing at the edge of the pool, laps water with a rapid tongue motion.

Wahs do not like to wade or even to get wet. Lee S. Crandall, for many years a curator at the Bronx Zoo, writes:

> They showed a definite distaste for wetting themselves, and when, apparently by accident, one got too far into the pool, it hastily scrambled out and shook itself with vigor, lifting its feet gingerly like a cat.

Foods and Feeding

While many mammals are bamboo foragers, few subsist on it. For the wah, bamboo is a main food source. Leaves and shoots of some half dozen or more kinds of bamboo make up the bulk of its diet.

Bamboos are woody-stemmed and have complex branching (more than one branch) at each of their nodes, or stem swellings. They spread by a system of rhizomes, or root stems. Their flowering cycle is long, as long as forty years.

Some kinds, like the umbrella bamboo, grow on lower mountain slopes. They are tall, thick-stemmed, and grow in clumps. Even though their branched rhizomes spread slowly, these shade-growing bamboos form extensive areas of forest undergrowth.

Higher up on mountain slopes arrow bamboo thrives. Its long rhizomes enable it to spread rapidly, but it is intolerant of shade and grows only in open glades, where its thin stems form dense ranks.

A wah feeds while standing or sitting on its haunches. It reaches out with a forepaw to grasp a bamboo stalk, bending it down so that the leaves are within reach. On the inside of each wrist is a hard, round nubbin formed by a small bone called the **radial sesamoid.*** Aligned with one of the small bones of the wrist, the wah's sesamoid connects to the long abductor muscle of the forelimb and has a slight degree of independent movement.

This same radial sesamoid is the giant panda's "thumb," an inch-and-a-half-long sixth digit it uses for grasping bamboo stalks. While the wah's forepaw is not nearly so specialized as the big panda's, its clasp is firm.

The wah reaches up and its forepaw enfolds a bamboo stem. Secured in the furred groove between the sesamoid knob and the pad of the first digit, the stem is raised to the side of the mouth. With quick head pulls it shears off leaf after leaf, chewing each mouthful extensively with its head slightly raised.

Collection and examination of scats reveals what a wah eats. In the Wolong Reserve shoots of umbrella bamboo are springtime food. Winter-collected scats are composed of finely chewed leaves. The Nepal study also involves scat collection. There the wahs feed on

---

*A sesamoid is a bone in a tendon, such as the kneecap. Radial refers to this sesamoid's position on the inner side of the lower forelimb.

leaves in early summer. Later in summer they eat shoots and leaves of ringal and red bamboos, supplemented by mushrooms. Their fall foods are bamboo leaves and *Sorbus* berries.

Unlike raccoons that live where there is cold and snow, red pandas have no need to den up in winter to avoid a time of food scarcity. Nor do they put on body fat for winter sustenance. For them, bamboo is a constant, year-round food source.

For energy to supply this continual leafy growth, bamboos rely on nutrients stored in their roots. Leaves are most tender and highest in nutrients in late summer and early fall, weaning time for wah cubs. When winter comes, the feathery tips of bamboo, weighed down by heavy snow, freeze to the ground. Then, even for the wah, a bamboo thicket is an impenetrable forest.

Bamboos are subject to die-offs. After many decades of growing, bamboos burst into bloom. Flowering may involve patches, small valleys, an entire mountainside, or an even larger area. Flowering shoots replace leafy shoots. The plants' nutrients are used up in this process. With no leafy shoots for photosynthesis, sugars are not replenished. Within a few months the bamboos die. A year later bamboo seeds sprout, but it is several years or more before the new bamboo plants are a food source.

While die-offs affect the panda's food supply, usually only one kind of bamboo flowers and dies at a given time. So wahs, unless they are restricted by clear-cut areas, can move on to seek another kind of bamboo. And there are other foods a wah eats. Bark and fruits of maples and beeches, as well as fungi and grasses, supplement its diet.

Wahs pluck blossoms and berries by reaching a forepaw or neatly nipping with incisor teeth. They relish mulberries. In captivity a wah sometimes rolls onto its back, as a kinkajou does, to savor a juicy grape.

Wahs, when they have the chance, are carnivorous. Sometimes they eat insects or snatch and kill a mouse or a bamboo rat. Bird eggs and nestlings are now-and-then finds. A captive wah may be quick enough to pounce on a hapless sparrow that flits into its enclosure, but in general wahs are not efficient predators.

Sometimes wahs are attracted to an unusual food source. Brian Houghton Hodgson notes their fondness for milk and ghee (butter boiled to an oil like consistency):

> [they] make their way furtively into remote dairies and cowherds' cottages to possess themselves of these luxuries.

The wah, like raccoons and other carnivores that are largely plant or fruit eaters, forages slowly through its forest habitat. In fact, an opportunistic **omnivore,** the red panda is regarded as a **folivore** (leaf eater) because it feeds mostly on bamboo leaves.

Wahs do exhibit characteristics of folivores in general. They are densely furred to conserve body heat. They have small-sized home ranges. They depend upon concealment to avoid predators. They have small litters. Their cubs are relatively slow developers. And, although they live much of their lives alone, wahs have a well-developed system of communication.

John Eisenberg, a zoologist at the University of Florida in Gainesville, writes of folivory, or leaf eating:

The utilization of leaves and stems, as a relatively complete source of energy, requires considerable morphological change, in dentition, jaw musculature, and gut morphology.

The panda fits into the third of Eisenberg's five classes of folivores: its teeth are modified for crushing leaves; its digestive tract is little modified from the basic carnivore plan; and, in addition to some animal food, it often feeds on other plant parts—buds, shoots, even grasses.

A wah's teeth, thirty-six or thirty-eight (if the individual has a fourth lower premolar), are modified for eating bamboo. While its incisors and canines look like those of other carnivores, the cheek

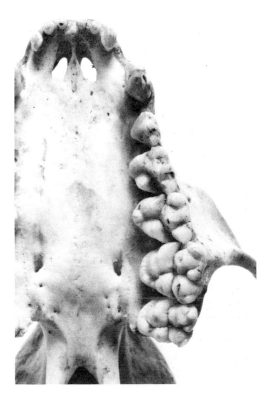

teeth, premolars and molars, are large and have high-cusped crowns for crushing and grinding. The panda has no carnassial shear, the meat-cutting device formed by last upper premolar and first lower molar in most of the carnivores.

The lower jaw, or **mandible,** is heavily ridged. The horizontal teeth-bearing part of the **ramus** (half of the jaw) is relatively short in proportion to the vertical extension with its high-arching coronoid process that serves for attachment of the **temporal** muscle that raises the jaw. Sturdy transverse condyles articulate jaw to skull. The chin's **symphysis** (joining) allows the two halves of the jaw a slight degree of independent movement. In chewing, each half moves side to side, effectively crushing tough fibrous plant material.

The wah has a robust skull that is large for a carnivore its size. Depth of skull gives greater bite pressure to the chewing teeth. Anatomist Theodore Grand points to the "deformation" of the panda skull that correlates with the powerfully developed chewing muscles. The skull is ridged and scarred. Widely flared, highly arched **zygomatic arches** (cheekbones) are the framework for another chewing muscle, the **masseter.** Again comparing red panda and raccoon,

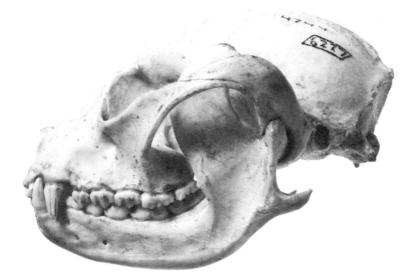

Grand weighed the musculature of the heads and found the panda has about twice as much skull muscle, most of it masticatory, or chewing, in function.

Anatomically a carnivore, the wah has a simple stomach and relatively short intestines. It lacks a chambered stomach or an intestinal pouch, adaptations found in many plant eaters for fermenting or absorbing nutrients. Unable to derive nutrients from the cellulose that makes up plant-cell walls, the wah relies on plant-cell content.

How then does the red panda thrive on a food source that is low in nutrients? Brian McNab, also at the University of Florida in Gainesville, is an authority on the energetics of folivores, having investigated the physiological problems and the ecological consequences of their reliance on an ever-available food supply.

Folivores tend to be relatively large, weighing one to five kilograms (about two to eleven pounds). Their body size is an adaptation for consuming a bulky leaf diet. The wah, if considered a folivore, is one of the largest. In captivity it consumes as much as one to one-and-a-half kilograms (about two to three pounds) of bamboo a night. Even so, only so many leaves can be ingested and processed in a night of foraging. All the folivores, Brian McNab finds, have a low **basal metabolism rate (BMR).** With lowered energy requirements, they are able to subsist on a low-energy food source.

Reduction in metabolism may also be an energy-saving strategy against the cold. While a thick coat and furred paws help to retain a wah's body heat, it may be that there is also a reduction in peripheral circulation in very cold weather. If this is so, speculates George Schaller, it would correlate with the activity pattern he observed for Jiao in the Wolong Reserve, and perhaps for her seemingly sluggish movements after periods of resting.

Mating

Increasing **photoperiod,** the gradual lengthening of daylight hours that commences in early winter, triggers sexual activity in wahs. The male pauses frequently to waddle, depositing his scent on rocks, logs, and branches. At mating time in the wild a male scent-marks to stake his territory, an area that may overlap the home ranges of two or more females. His scent posts are warnings to other males.

Although mating can occur from late fall into spring, the male's testes are retained in the abdomen until early January. This limiting of the time during which viable sperm are produced restricts conception to a two-month period, mid-January to mid-March. In turn it insures that cubbing is clustered within a two-month period, June and July.

During the mating season, male and female sleep close to each other in a tree. Sometimes their bodies touch. They come down to feed together. First one scent-marks, then the other. Occasionally they twitter-call back and forth. The male trails the female, nose to tail. She flicks her tail and bounds away. Eventually the wahs mate.

4

Cubs

When the rainy season begins in early summer, bamboos produce shoots and trees and shrubs flower and bear fruits. With an abundance of foods, pandas restrict their foraging to smaller areas. And females search for suitable dens. June and July are cubbing months.

On July 2 Pralad Yonzon's radio-collared female 102 denned in the hollow of a dead fir tree. Two days later, female 103 found and entered another fir-tree hollow. Suspecting that both pandas had moved into nursery dens, and not wanting to disturb them, Yonzon was careful to observe from a distance.

Dens

Tree cavities and sometimes rock crevices are selected for nursery dens in the wild. According to Brian Houghton Hodgson, the female wah "brings forth [her cubs] amid the recesses of the rocks in spring or early summer." Zoo pandas seem content with den boxes on the ground. At the National Zoo each wooden box has a slanted square tile, just big enough for a wah to squeeze through, that makes a weatherproof opening and a hinged top, so that cubs can be checked or fresh hay put in.

Before Cubbing

A month before cubbing the female appears heavy and somewhat lethargic. Resting in a tree she frequently adjusts her position. She is most comfortable stretched out on a limb.

Two weeks before cubbing the eight teats become noticeable on her sparsely furred underside. A week later she shows interest in the den boxes. She gathers sticks and grass, bites off leaves and small twigs, and carries them by the mouthful into one den, and then another.

A choice of dens is necessary because a mother wah, when anxious or alarmed, moves her cubs. If another den is not available, she carries the cub about in her mouth, behavior that stresses both cubs and mother. For all the female's nursery preparations, the nest for her cubs will be a round depression just the size of her curled body.

In the early 1940s the San Diego Zoo had breeding success with its wahs. Keeper Georgie Dittoc readied a nest box and filled it with clean straw:

> Whiteface took to her nest [on June 3] where she sat bolt upright all day, a grave and patient look on her little face. I left her reluctantly, long after quitting time that night, and hurried to see her as soon as it was light in the morning. Sure enough there were two whitish bundles of fur beside her.

Birth

A few days before cubbing, the female is restless. She scent-marks often and grooms herself. Random pacing occurs just before she gives birth. Some 134 days after mating, a long **gestation,** the cubs are born. Usually there are two, sometimes just one, rarely three or four cubs in a litter.

Parturition, the birth process, may be quick (two cubs within ten minutes), or several hours may elapse between the appearance of the babies. Miles Roberts has found litters of just one newborn on the morning check and later in the day discovered two or more cubs had been born.

As each cub begins to emerge, the female starts to lick it. She may even open the **amniotic sac.** Once the cub is all the way out of her birth canal, the mother consumes this membrane as well as the umbilical cord and placenta. Her vigorous head-to-tail-and-toes licking stimulates the cub's circulation. Ten minutes after birth, a cub is clean and fluffy dry.

In 1908 Major F. Wall had a look at two-day-old wah cubs, a male and a female, born to a wild-caught wah in the Darjeeling Horticulture Gardens. He comments on their mother's tameness:

> While the attendant extracted the cubs from their nest she squatted on a beam just above our heads, . . . and then she attentively watched . . . [she] showed no distress for her little ones . . .

Then he describes the infants:

> . . . the markings which contribute to the quaint character of the adult faces [were] altogether absent . . . [and] there was no trace of the red rings which encircle the tail.

Scent recognition is important in the mother-cub bonding that occurs after birth. Miles Roberts managed to put a still-wet abandoned cub with another female's litter. He first rubbed the cub with feces found in the foster wah's enclosure, then rubbed the cub against the small furry forms of her own cubs. Then he placed the cub in the nest with its foster siblings. A check six hours later found the cub fluffy. The female had cleaned and dried it and accepted it as her own.

Sound also plays a role in bonding. On another occasion Roberts found a newborn, one of two cubs, that had been dropped outside the den box. Using gloves smeared with the mother's feces, he picked up the infant. When it *wheeet*-called in distress, he put it in the den entrance. Immediately the mother left the other cub, sniffed the foundling, picked it up in her mouth, carried it around the enclosure, and then took it back into the den where she cleaned and fed it.

A litter, if there is more than one cub, almost always contains both sexes. Small litters (two or one) tend to have a higher survival rate than large litters (three or four). Inbreeding also affects mortality. Offspring of a closely related pair have a lower survival rate than cubs of pandas that are distant relatives or not related at all.

In 1972 the red pandas at the National Zoo produced the first babies that survived to become adults. Since then, under Miles Roberts's guidance, the wah population has swelled. More than 100 cubs have been born at the zoo, most of them eventually placed in other zoos around the world.

A Cub Named Nicholas

Sometimes a cub is rejected by its mother or appears not to be thriving in her care. Then zoo curators and keepers face a difficult decision: whether to wait and see if the mother does assume care or to remove and hand rear the infant.

Nicholas is an orphan cub at the National Zoo. He fell from his mother's grasp when he was very small and was found on the ground by the keeper.

There are other orphans in the zoo's hand-rearing facility, but Nicholas is the only red panda. It is obvious the staff likes him and takes special care of him.

At forty-three days, Nick's soft baby fur is interspersed with red guard hairs. Blackish hairs have grown in on his lower body and legs. His ears are softly tufted and his tail bands and tear tracks are darkening.

Every seven hours Nicholas is fed. On the scale, after a feeding, he weighs 720 grams (about 25 ounces). This indicates that Nicholas, who weighed 700 grams just before feeding, took 20 cubic centimeters of Esbilac formula.

After feeding and weighing, Nicholas is carried about on a shoulder, gently patted on the back so that he burps and gets rid of any swallowed air. Then he is gently returned to the soft, rumpled towel that is his nest. Within a few seconds little Nick is asleep.

At the National Zoo

The panda enclosure is ideal habitat. Large (2,600 square feet), it has live trees and shrubs, a pool with running water, and natural substrate, soil and grass. Wahs feel at home. And they feel secure because tall shrubs and growing bamboo screen three sides of the

enclosure. Panda viewing is restricted to a low-fenced, deep-moated side of the yard.

On July 13 cubs are born to Eunice and Herb, the resident panda pair. For much of the first week Eunice stays close to her two babies. She spends hours at a time in the den with them, then rests nearby on a low branch of the mulberry tree or feeds on bamboo. Herb, high up in the tree, or feeding on the ground, is often the only panda to be seen.

Fully furred at birth, the cubs weigh 120 grams (just over 4 ounces). From nose to tail tip they measure 280 millimeters (not quite 11 inches). Their eyes and their ear openings are sealed.

Eunice soon resumes her usual resting periods in the tree. Her week-old infants no longer require constant attention. The cubs have each other. Most of the time they sleep, their small bodies pressed together. Litter contact provides comfort as well as shared warmth.

When Eunice visits the den, she twitters to her cubs, then curls on her side or sits over them while they suckle. Small forepaws tread against her belly as they nurse. She licks one cub, then the other to stimulate elimination. By consuming both urine and feces, she keeps the nursery den clean and free from odors that, in the wild, might attract a passing predator. Sometimes Eunice curls her body around the cubs and naps.

Wah cubs develop slowly. In fact, for their body size they are

among the slowest developing of all the carnivores. During the first weeks thick, woolly, gray-buff fur covers their small, pink-skinned bodies. Their paw pads are bare. By the end of the second week red guard hairs appear, giving a reddish tinge to the fur on their backs. Black guard hairs grow in to darken undersides and legs. At three weeks their eyes and ears are open. At six weeks their tiny tear tracks are defined, their tails are banded, and their paws are furred. At two months the cubs look like little wahs. Teaser is noticeably larger than his sister, Firecat.

Feeding the Cubs

For a female red panda, as for any mammal mother, **lactation** (the supplying of milk for her babies) is a time of stress, when energy costs to her body are high.

John Gittleman undertook a study of how the wah's low-energy food (bamboo) affects development of cubs and maternal care. Daily observations began in May in two panda enclosures, each the habitat of a breeding pair. Cubs were born in early July. But even before cubbing occurred, the nursery dens were monitored through red-tinted Plexiglas windows that kept out light and made it possible to check the nest without disturbing the pandas.

Jill Garnett assisted in the project. She used check sheets, with behavioral categories outlined on them, to record her observations. Even on rainy days Jill watched the wahs. And twice a day, when he came to tend the pandas, Keeper Steve Clevenger added his observations of what the wahs were doing.

After the cubs were born, the team closely monitored their devel-

opment. Little Firecat watches anxiously as John Gittleman carefully removes her brother from the den box for weighing and a close-up inspection.

To determine how a **lactating** (nursing) female panda manages to provide milk for her cubs and meet her own energetic needs on a diet of mostly bamboo, the study focused on four feeding characteristics: duration of feeding at a bamboo stalk, number of leaves per mouthful, interval between mouthfuls of leaves, and total number of leaves eaten per minute.

This is what John Gittleman found. A female when lactating feeds for a longer time—from about five minutes to an average of fifteen minutes at a stalk. She also increases the leaves eaten per minute, from seven to an average of twenty. But "the most dramatic behavioral change," according to Gittleman, is the increase in number of leaves per mouthful, from one leaf to three or four leaves. Given a low-nutrient diet and her relatively inadequate ability to process plant foods, a mother wah increases her bamboo consumption by gorging on leaves.

John Gittleman suspects that the energetic demands during reproduction limit litter size to two cubs or just one. And he thinks the reason a mother wah spends only brief times in the nursery den is because her nutritionally poor diet results in low milk production. Probably the cubs' own slow rate of development is a consequence of getting relatively little milk and even that is of low-nutrient quality.

Outside the Den

By September Teaser and Firecat are replicas of their parents and
weigh about two and a half pounds. They spend many of their waking
hours pouncing and climbing over each other in the nest or investigating the den entrance. When Eunice is not watching, they poke their
heads out of the tile doorway. A ground den has a safety advantage
at this stage. A mother wah in the wild, with cubs in a tree den, must
worry, unless she has moved them to a ground den to prevent tum-
bles. The cubs' first forays out of the den occur at night, and they do
not venture far from the den.

Once the cubs discover the world outside the den, they make life difficult for their mother. Again and again she returns them to the nest, only to have them reappear.

But cubs also can be difficult about coming out of the den. One day, as Jill Garnett looks on, Eunice coaxes Firecat and Teaser out of the nest box. She stands in the tile opening, waiting expectantly for the cubs to join her. She comes out and looks over her shoulder to see if they are following. But the cubs have retreated into the nest. Again and again Eunice tries to entice them to come out. She is an experienced mother, firm with discipline. Back she goes into the den and pushes one of the cubs out. The cub turns and scurries back in. Finally she gets Firecat out. Then Teaser, wanting to join his sister, makes a small flying leap and lands on the ground.

Within a few weeks the cubs trail their mother. Often they follow her to the edge of the pool where there are fresh bamboo branches. They press together and stay close to her heels. While their mother

feeds, the cubs sample leaves and grass and climb on the big rock. After twenty minutes Eunice leads them back to the den box.

Soon the cubs are agile climbers. Much of the time they rest where Eunice does, follow her down from the mulberry tree, feed when she feeds, or play near her, batting at twigs and leaves, and tussling with each other.

The cubs are adept now at manipulating bamboo stems. And they are curious. Eunice is still very protective. When a cub strays, or becomes frightened, its *wheeet* call brings its mother running. If Eunice senses danger, she lures the cubs away by running past them. If they do not follow her, she nudges their small rumps or bites their necks to head them off.

Play is a now-and-then preoccupation for Firecat and Teaser. It involves the perfecting of pouncing, wrestling, chasing, biting, as well as climbing and swatting, actions a cub one day will use in encounters with other adult wahs. Aggressive displays, prey-capture techniques, and escape tactics all are practiced in play. And all these actions are executed with energy and exuberance, as the cubs experiment in judging distances, running to overtake or cut each other off, and how to land forepaw strikes. The cubs gain coordination and fitness as they play. Alternately attack becomes defense, fighting turns to "prey killing." The victim of one bout becomes the victor in the next skirmish.

Teaser invites Firecat to play with a head shake and flicks of his tail. Sometimes she ignores the invitation. But often a wrestling bout

ensues. Teaser pounces, biting and swatting. Then the cubs chase. First he chases Firecat, then she turns and pursues him. Biting and scratching is restrained. Teaser stands tall on his hind legs, his forearms upraised, and snorts—a threat gesture executed in play.

By late fall the cubs are more independent. Once in a while Eunice joins in their play, or even initiates it. More often she ignores their play gestures. But occasionally she still allows a cub to suckle while she grooms it.

Although nutritionally weaned and capable of living on their own, Firecat and Teaser, like wah cubs in the wild, stay with their mother through their first winter. On very cold days all four pandas shelter in the den box, where their furred forms provide shared warmth. On most days three curled balls, cubs and mother, huddle high in the branches of one fork, while Herb maintains his sleeping place in the other fork of the mulberry.

Herb, who has been aloof from the cubs, begins to join in their wrestling bouts. Usually he plays with Teaser, the male cub, while Firecat looks on or amuses herself by running around. At first Herb's participation is in play. Later in winter it becomes a prelude to the mating season.

Miles Roberts suggests that by interacting with the cubs at a time when "tensions between the female and the young may be high," the male gradually gets closer to the female. Sometimes Herb gives voice to his emotions with a plaintive whinnylike *we-ee-ee-oo*. However it is, in late winter the adult wahs are preoccupied with each other. Social weaning of the cubs takes place as Herb and Eunice ignore or even are hostile to their nearly adult-sized offspring.

From late February on, Teaser and Firecat are increasingly independent. They rest together, climb about in the mulberry together, and even forage on the ground together.

By spring wah cubs in the wild disperse and eventually establish their own home ranges. It is time for Firecat and Teaser to be moved to the Conservation and Research Center at Front Royal.

In a month or so Eunice will be investigating the hollow log and the den boxes, while Herb will be resting in his favorite fork of the mulberry tree.

A Final Word

"In their general appearance the wahs are quite unique." So writes Brian Houghton Hodgson, the man who lived with wahs nearly a century and a half ago. Except for their "short sharp visage and eminently bland expression of countenance . . . they might be described like the Raccoons as small Bears with long tails."

With their beauty of color, pattern, and form it is little wonder that Hodgson admired wahs. At a loss to adequately describe his favorite animals, he concludes that "to be apprehended they must be seen."

GLOSSARY

ADAPTATION: an inherited characteristic—behavioral, structural, or functional—that fits an animal (or plant) for its habitat

AGONISTIC ENCOUNTER: a meeting that involves attack, defense, or submission

AMNIOTIC SAC: embryonic membrane that surrounds a developing mammal

ARBOREAL: living in trees

AUDITORY BULLAE: hollow, rounded tympanic-bone enlargements that contain the middle ear

BASAL METABOLISM RATE (BMR): the minimum amount of energy required to maintain life at normal body temperature; usually measured by oxygen consumption

BIPEDAL: standing on two feet

CARNIVORES: mammals that belong to the order Carnivora; also used to refer to meat eaters

CONIFEROUS: cone-bearing

CONVERGENT: adjective that describes a character (or characters) developed through time in two different groups of animals, usually in response to similarity in habits or environment

CREPUSCULAR: active in twilight or before sunrise

CRYPTIC: concealing

DECIDUOUS: leaf-shedding

DISPERSAL: the movement of a young animal from the area in which it was born, or of an adult animal from one area to another

FLEHMEN: the facial grimace associated with olfactory perception

FOLIVORES: animals that eat leaves

GENETIC VARIABILITY: diversity of the functional hereditary units, the genes, in a population

GESTATION: the period from conception to birth

HOME RANGE: the area over which an animal roams in the course of its normal activities

INBREEDING: the mating of kin

LACTATING: nursing

LACTATION: the secretion of milk

MANDIBLE: the lower jaw

MASSETER: a chewing muscle that has its origin on the zygomatic arch of the skull and its insertion on the lower jaw

MUSTELIDS: members of the family Mustelidae (weasels, otters, skunks, badgers)

NOCTURNAL: active at night

OMNIVORES: animals that eat both plant and animal foods

PARTURITION: the process of giving birth

PHEROMONE: a substance released by an animal, which affects the behavioral response of other animals of the same species

PHOTOPERIOD: the duration of daylight in relation to darkness over a twenty-four-hour period

PROCYONIDAE: the family of raccoons and their relatives (ringtail, coati, kinkajou, olingo, and, possibly, the red panda)

PROCYONIDS: members of the raccoon family, the Procyonidae

RADIAL SESAMOID: a small bone, present in some carnivores and sometimes enlarged, on the radial or inner side of the wrist

RAMUS: one of the paired bones that form the lower jaw, or mandible

RAPTOR: bird of prey (hawk or owl)

SCANSORIAL: capable of climbing

SCATS: an animal's feces or droppings

SCAT STATIONS: places used repeatedly for defecation

SEMIPLANTIGRADE: not quite flat-footed; the heel of the hind foot rarely contacts the ground

SYMPHYSIS: the more or less movable union of two bones

TEMPORAL MUSCLE: a chewing muscle that has its origin on the temporal bone of the skull and its insertion on the coronoid process of the lower jaw

URSIDS: members of the family Ursidae (bears and, according to some scientists, both the pandas)

VIVERRIDS: members of the family Viverridae (mongooses, civets, genets)

VOMERONASAL ORGAN: a small sensory pit in the roof of the mouth

ZYGOMATIC ARCHES: the cheekbones

REFERENCES

Bartlett, A. D. *Wild Beasts in the "Zoo."* London: Chapman and Hall, 1900.

Crandall, Lee S. *The Management of Wild Mammals in Captivity.* Chicago: University of Chicago Press, 1964.

Davis, Joseph A. *Pandas.* New York: Curtis Books, 1973.

Eisenberg, John F. *The Mammalian Radiations.* Chicago: University of Chicago Press, 1981.

Ewer, R. F. *The Carnivores.* Ithaca, N.Y.: Cornell University Press, 1973.

Gittleman, John, and Jill Garnett. "The 'other' panda." *Zoogoer* 14 (1985):4–7.

Gittleman, John L., and Paul H. Harvey. "Carnivore home-range size, metabolic needs and ecology." *Behavioral Ecology and Sociobiology* 10 (1982):57–63.

Hardwicke, Thomas. "Description of a new genus of the Class Mammalia, from the Himalaya chain of hills between Nepaul [sic] and the snowy mountains." *Transactions of the Linnaean Society of London* 15 (1827):161–65.

Hodgson, B. H. "On the cat-toed subplantigrades of the sub-Himalayas." *Journal of the Asiatic Society of Bengal* 16 (1847):1113–29.

Hunter, W. W. *Life of Brian Houghton Hodgson.* London: John Murray, 1896.

McNab, Brian. "Energetics of arboreal folivores: Physiological consequences of feeding on a ubiquitous food supply." In *The Ecology of Arboreal Folivores,* edited by G. Montgomery. Washington, D.C.: Smithsonian Institution Press, 1978.

Morris, Ramona, and Desmond Morris. *Men and Pandas.* New York: McGraw-Hill, 1966.

Roberts, Miles S. "Growth and development of mother-reared red pandas." *International Zoo Yearbook* 15 (1975):57–63.

———. "The fire fox." *Animal Kingdom* 85 (1982):20–27.

———, and John L. Gittleman. *"Ailurus fulgens." Mammalian Species* 222 (1984):1–8.

———, and David S. Kessler. "Reproduction in red pandas, *Ailurus fulgens* (Carnivora: Ailuropodidae)." *Journal of Zoology* 188 (1979):235–49.

Schaller, George B., Hu Jinchu, Pan Wenshi, and Zhu Jing. *The Giant Pandas of Wolong.* Chicago: University of Chicago Press, 1985.

Sowerby, Arthur de C. "The pandas or cat-bears." *The China Journal* 17 (1932):296–99.

Tedford, R. H., and E. P. Gustafson. "First North American record of the extinct panda *Parailurus." Nature* 265 (1977):621–23.

ACKNOWLEDGMENTS

First of all, our admiration and gratitude go to the red pandas themselves—Tarzan, Herb and Eunice, Firecat, Teaser, Pooka and Bartholomew at the National Zoo, and Li Ning and Tong Fei at the Bronx Zoo. We are also indebted to a number of people for their interest and help. Miles S. Roberts, Department of Zoological Research at the National Zoo, and Dr. John L. Gittleman, Department of Zoology, University of Tennessee, shared their knowledge of wahs and their ways and their enthusiasm for their animals. We especially thank them both.

Dr. Patricia D. Moehlman, an authority on carnivores, put us in touch with her colleague in Nepal, Pralad Yonzon. Dr. George B. Schaller was generous in providing information on the wahs in the Wolong Reserve. Kay M. Schaller shared her impressions of China and Nepal and also supplied Chinese names we intended to use in place of Herb and Eunice.

James G. Doherty, general curator at the New York Zoological Park (Bronx Zoo), introduced us to his newly acquired Li Ning and Tong Fei and supplied accounts of their introduction to the Himalayan Highlands exhibit area.

Jill Garnett, who assisted Dr. Gittleman at the National Zoo, furnished several on-the-spot accounts from her devoted hours of wah watching. Keeper Steve Clevenger kept us posted on cub activity and with his knowledge of the care and feeding of pandas contributed much to our photographic success.

Dr. Theodore I. Grand, also of the National Zoo's Department of Zoological Research, discussed some of his work on the anatomy of pandas and raccoons.

Peter Haller translated a paper from the German. Evelyn Haller proved an able assistant on a cold late-winter trek to Himalayan Highlands.

Information on the watercolor sketches by Brian Houghton Hodgson came from R. Fish, Librarian of the Zoological Society of London. Professor B. Elizabeth Horner, ever supportive of our projects, found an important paper on climbing adaptations while pursuing her own interests in the Smith College science library.

William K. Sacco, Chief Photographer at the Peabody Museum of Natural History, Yale University, prepared photographs from old journals and from museum specimens. We are also grateful to Copeland MacClintock and to Andrew L. Young for their support and for their comments on text and photographs.

Yale University's Kline Science Library once again proved to be a trove of scientific information, and its staff librarians were most helpful in tracking the early accounts of red pandas.

DM and EY

INDEX